I M A G E S

IMAGES

ROBERT JAMES WALLER

WARNER BOOKS

A TIME WARNER COMPANY

Copyright © 1994 Robert James Waller

Warner Book, Inc., 1271 Avenue of the Americas, New York, NY 10020

⟪W⟫ A Time Warner Company

Printed in the United States of America

First Printing: July 1994

10 9 8 7 6 5 4 3 2 1

Library of Congress Cataloging-in-Publication Data

Waller, Robert James

Images / Robert James Waller.

p. cm.

ISBN 0-446-67031-6

1. Iowa—Pictorial works. 2. Madison County (Iowa)—Pictorial works.

3. Bridges—Iowa—Madison County—Pictorial works.

I. Title

F622.W34 1994

977.7'81033'0222—dc20   94-2095

CIP

FOREWORD

I do not have a particular photographic specialty and therefore shoot whatever catches my eye at a particular moment. Much of the time I deal in somewhat offbeat, abstract images. The postcards in this book, however, are straightforward landscapes of Iowa and the bridges of Madison County. They are mostly scenes that jumped out at me while wandering around Iowa in my truck.

As I look at them, I can recall the exact moment when I hit the shutter—the time of day, what the weather was like, and where I was, not only geographically but also in my mind. A woman brought me blueberry muffins at dawn one morning, and I photographed a river sunrise thirty minutes later, stamping my feet to keep them warm in November cold. Late October was particularly nice in 1989, and I spent a week in the countryside of south Iowa where several of these shots were made. And the deer—I'll never forget them—I startled them at twilight while walking along a creek in northwest

Iowa. They ran in a long semicircle before pausing on the ridge of a plowed field. It took an eight-second exposure on Kodachrome 25 to get the shot. One of them moved slightly, giving me a "ghost image."

On another occasion I was only a hundred yards from home in a swampy area, mist rising over small ponds at dawn. I hustled back to the house and awakened my wife, bribing her with a cup of coffee and asking her if she'd pose for me. She only complained a little as I took her through long, wet grass to one of the ponds. A solitary muskrat used the pond that summer, but it dried up the following year during a drought, and I sometimes wonder whatever happened to the little fellow.

For me, then, these photographs evoke memories of early morning fog in April, late October twilights, and driving into some country town an hour after sunset when all the restaurants were closed and supper came down to whatever was left in my cooler—bread, cheese, and fruit, usually. And, certainly, some of the photos evoke the quiet times I have spent with the bridges of Madison County before the world discovered them. I suspect they will be quiet once again, next year or maybe the year after that. And I will be there in my knee-high rubber boots, standing in the riffles of a small stream, looking at the bridges down my lenses.

This is Iowa, then, the place where I live. I hope you enjoy traveling with me and thinking about how and why I made these photographs. I was usually alone, but not lonely, especially when photographing the bridges, for they are alive in their own way, a way I cannot describe in words. But if you're around the bridges at dawn or in the gray rains of a September afternoon and listening, you can almost hear them breathing . . . almost.

Cedar Falls, Iowa
February 1994

ROBERT JAMES WALLER · IMAGES ·

BY THE AUTHOR OF THE BRIDGES OF MADISON COUNTY

PLACE
STAMP
HERE

ROBERT JAMES WALLER

BY THE
AUTHOR OF
THE BRIDGES
OF MADISON
COUNTY

ROBERT JAMES WALLER · IMAGES

ROBERT JAMES WALLER

BY THE
AUTHOR OF
THE BRIDGES
OF MADISON
COUNTY

· IMAGES ·

OLD POST OFFICE—BENTONSPORT, IOWA. ©1994 ROBERT JAMES WALLER

ROBERT JAMES WALLER

BY THE
AUTHOR OF
THE BRIDGES
OF MADISON
COUNTY

ROBERT JAMES WALLER · IMAGES ·

LAMP IN WINDOW—BENTONSPORT, IOWA. ©1994 ROBERT JAMES WALLER

DAWN–GRUNDY COUNTY, IOWA. ©1994 ROBERT JAMES WALLER

ROBERT JAMES WALLER · IMAGES ·

BY THE
AUTHOR OF
THE BRIDGES
OF MADISON
COUNTY

YELLOW LEAF IN BLUE BOTTLE—BENTONSPORT, IOWA. ©1994 ROBERT JAMES WALLER

ROBERT JAMES WALLER

BY THE
AUTHOR OF
THE BRIDGES
OF MADISON
COUNTY

· IMAGES ·

ROBERT JAMES WALLER · IMAGES

BY THE AUTHOR OF THE BRIDGES OF MADISON COUNTY

THERE WERE GREEN MORNINGS, TOO—CEDAR FALLS, IOWA. ©1994 ROBERT JAMES WALLER

ROBERT JAMES WALLER · IMAGES

BY THE
AUTHOR OF
THE BRIDGES
OF MADISON
COUNTY

GRAIN TERMINAL—CLAYTON, IOWA. ©1994 ROBERT JAMES WALLER

ROBERT JAMES WALLER · IMAGES

ROBERT JAMES WALLER

BY THE AUTHOR OF THE BRIDGES OF MADISON COUNTY

ROBERT JAMES WALLER

BY THE
AUTHOR OF
THE BRIDGES
OF MADISON
COUNTY

· IMAGES ·

GRUNDY COUNTY, IOWA. ©1994 ROBERT JAMES WALLER

ROBERT JAMES WALLER · IMAGES ·

BY THE
AUTHOR OF
THE BRIDGES
OF MADISON
COUNTY

PLACE
STAMP
HERE

ROBERT JAMES WALLER · IMAGES

BY THE
AUTHOR OF
THE BRIDGES
OF MADISON
COUNTY

PLACE
STAMP
HERE

ROBERT JAMES WALLER

BY THE
AUTHOR OF
THE BRIDGES
OF MADISON
COUNTY

· IMAGES ·

PLACE

STAMP

HERE

ROBERT JAMES WALLER

BY THE AUTHOR OF THE BRIDGES OF MADISON COUNTY

· IMAGES ·

KEOSAUQUA, IOWA. ©1994 ROBERT JAMES WALLER

ROBERT JAMES WALLER · · IMAGES ·

BY THE
AUTHOR OF
THE BRIDGES
OF MADISON
COUNTY

ROBERT JAMES WALLER

BY THE
AUTHOR OF
THE BRIDGES
OF MADISON
COUNTY

· IMAGES ·

OLD SCHOOL HOUSE—NORTHEAST IOWA. ©1994 ROBERT JAMES WALLER

ROBERT JAMES WALLER · IMAGES ·

BY THE
AUTHOR OF
THE BRIDGES
OF MADISON
COUNTY

WINDMILL-AMANA COLONIES REGION (IOWA). ©1994 ROBERT JAMES WALLER

ROBERT JAMES WALLER · IMAGES

BY THE AUTHOR OF THE BRIDGES OF MADISON COUNTY

DUST STORM—CENTRAL IOWA. ©1994 ROBERT JAMES WALLER

ROBERT JAMES WALLER · IMAGES ·

BY THE AUTHOR OF THE BRIDGES OF MADISON COUNTY

ROBERT JAMES WALLER · IMAGES ·

BY THE AUTHOR OF THE BRIDGES OF MADISON COUNTY

PLACE STAMP HERE

SUN AND WIRE–CLAYTON COUNTY, IOWA. ©1994 ROBERT JAMES WALLER

CEDAR BRIDGE—MADISON COUNTY, IOWA. ©1994 ROBERT JAMES WALLER

ROBERT JAMES WALLER

BY THE
AUTHOR OF
THE BRIDGES
OF MADISON
COUNTY

· IMAGES ·

NINA'S LAWN—CEDAR FALLS, IOWA. ©1994 ROBERT JAMES WALLER

ROBERT JAMES WALLER · IMAGES ·

BY THE
AUTHOR OF
THE BRIDGES
OF MADISON
COUNTY

ONE GOOD ROAD IS ENOUGH—VAN BUREN COUNTY, IOWA.
©1994 ROBERT JAMES WALLER

PLACE

STAMP

HERE